BEEHIVE INSPECTION

Journal

INSPECTION CHECKLIST

Date: Time:

	HIVE 1	HIVE 2	HIVE 3	HIVE 4	HIVE 5	HIVE 6
GENERAL HIVE APPEARENCE						
Are the bee actively entering/ exiting the hive?						
Are the bees bringing in pollen?						
Are their signs of robbing?						
Are their signs an animal has been disturbing the hive?						
Are the bees calm when opening the hive? (otherwise it could indicate queenlessness, a poor weather, etc.)						
REPRODUCTION						
Is the brood pattern good? (otherwise it could indicate a disease or an unwell queen)						
Are larvae healthy, shiny and white?						
Is there royal jelly in cells with larva?						
Is there brood in capped or uncapped cells?						
Is there one egg or larva per cell?						
SIGNS OF PEST						
Mites test result (visual inspection only is insufficient)						
Are ants present?						
Are wax moths present?						
Is there an unusual amount of dead bees?						
Is there an odor?						
CAPACITY						
How many frames are covered in bees?						
How many cells are being fully (or almost fully) used for brood?						
Is there enough space to store nectar? (empty combs/space to build new combs)						
WEATHER						
Temperature/Precipitation						
Has there been a significant change in total population since the last inspection?						

NOTES

INSPECTION CHECKLIST

Date: Time:

	HIVE 1	HIVE 2	HIVE 3	HIVE 4	HIVE 5	HIVE 6
GENERAL HIVE APPEARENCE						
Are the bee actively entering/ exiting the hive?						
Are the bees bringing in pollen?						
Are their signs of robbing?						
Are their signs an animal has been disturbing the hive?						
Are the bees calm when opening the hive? (otherwise it could indicate queenlessness, a poor weather, etc.)						
REPRODUCTION						
Is the brood pattern good? (otherwise it could indicate a disease or an unwell queen)						
Are larvae healthy, shiny and white?						
Is there royal jelly in cells with larva?						
Is there brood in capped or uncapped cells?						
Is there one egg or larva per cell?						
SIGNS OF PEST						
Mites test result (visual inspection only is insufficient)						
Are ants present?						
Are wax moths present?						
Is there an unusual amount of dead bees?						
Is there an odor?						
CAPACITY						
How many frames are covered in bees?						
How many cells are being fully (or almost fully) used for brood?						
Is there enough space to store nectar? (empty combs/space to build new combs)						
WEATHER						
Temperature/Precipitation						
Has there been a significant change in total population since the last inspection?						

NOTES

INSPECTION CHECKLIST

Date: Time:

	HIVE 1	HIVE 2	HIVE 3	HIVE 4	HIVE 5	HIVE 6
GENERAL HIVE APPEARENCE						
Are the bee actively entering/ exiting the hive?						
Are the bees bringing in pollen?						
Are their signs of robbing?						
Are their signs an animal has been disturbing the hive?						
Are the bees calm when opening the hive? (otherwise it could indicate queenlessness, a poor weather, etc.)						
REPRODUCTION						
Is the brood pattern good? (otherwise it could indicate a disease or an unwell queen)						
Are larvae healthy, shiny and white?						
Is there royal jelly in cells with larva?						
Is there brood in capped or uncapped cells?						
Is there one egg or larva per cell?						
SIGNS OF PEST						
Mites test result (visual inspection only is insufficient)						
Are ants present?						
Are wax moths present?						
Is there an unusual amount of dead bees?						
Is there an odor?						
CAPACITY						
How many frames are covered in bees?						
How many cells are being fully (or almost fully) used for brood?						
Is there enough space to store nectar? (empty combs/space to build new combs)						
WEATHER						
Temperature/Precipitation						
Has there been a significant change in total population since the last inspection?						

NOTES

INSPECTION CHECKLIST

Date: Time:

	HIVE 1	HIVE 2	HIVE 3	HIVE 4	HIVE 5	HIVE 6
GENERAL HIVE APPEARENCE						
Are the bee actively entering/ exiting the hive?						
Are the bees bringing in pollen?						
Are their signs of robbing?						
Are their signs an animal has been disturbing the hive?						
Are the bees calm when opening the hive? (otherwise it could indicate queenlessness, a poor weather, etc.)						
REPRODUCTION						
Is the brood pattern good? (otherwise it could indicate a disease or an unwell queen)						
Are larvae healthy, shiny and white?						
Is there royal jelly in cells with larva?						
Is there brood in capped or uncapped cells?						
Is there one egg or larva per cell?						
SIGNS OF PEST						
Mites test result (visual inspection only is insufficient)						
Are ants present?						
Are wax moths present?						
Is there an unusual amount of dead bees?						
Is there an odor?						
CAPACITY						
How many frames are covered in bees?						
How many cells are being fully (or almost fully) used for brood?						
Is there enough space to store nectar? (empty combs/space to build new combs)						
WEATHER						
Temperature/Precipitation						
Has there been a significant change in total population since the last inspection?						

NOTES

INSPECTION CHECKLIST

Date: Time:

	HIVE 1	HIVE 2	HIVE 3	HIVE 4	HIVE 5	HIVE 6
GENERAL HIVE APPEARENCE						
Are the bee actively entering/ exiting the hive?						
Are the bees bringing in pollen?						
Are their signs of robbing?						
Are their signs an animal has been disturbing the hive?						
Are the bees calm when opening the hive? (otherwise it could indicate queenlessness, a poor weather, etc.)						
REPRODUCTION						
Is the brood pattern good? (otherwise it could indicate a disease or an unwell queen)						
Are larvae healthy, shiny and white?						
Is there royal jelly in cells with larva?						
Is there brood in capped or uncapped cells?						
Is there one egg or larva per cell?						
SIGNS OF PEST						
Mites test result (visual inspection only is insufficient)						
Are ants present?						
Are wax moths present?						
Is there an unusual amount of dead bees?						
Is there an odor?						
CAPACITY						
How many frames are covered in bees?						
How many cells are being fully (or almost fully) used for brood?						
Is there enough space to store nectar? (empty combs/space to build new combs)						
WEATHER						
Temperature/Precipitation						
Has there been a significant change in total population since the last inspection?						

NOTES

INSPECTION CHECKLIST

Date: Time:

	HIVE 1	HIVE 2	HIVE 3	HIVE 4	HIVE 5	HIVE 6
GENERAL HIVE APPEARENCE						
Are the bee actively entering/ exiting the hive?						
Are the bees bringing in pollen?						
Are their signs of robbing?						
Are their signs an animal has been disturbing the hive?						
Are the bees calm when opening the hive? (otherwise it could indicate queenlessness, a poor weather, etc.)						
REPRODUCTION						
Is the brood pattern good? (otherwise it could indicate a disease or an unwell queen)						
Are larvae healthy, shiny and white?						
Is there royal jelly in cells with larva?						
Is there brood in capped or uncapped cells?						
Is there one egg or larva per cell?						
SIGNS OF PEST						
Mites test result (visual inspection only is insufficient)						
Are ants present?						
Are wax moths present?						
Is there an unusual amount of dead bees?						
Is there an odor?						
CAPACITY						
How many frames are covered in bees?						
How many cells are being fully (or almost fully) used for brood?						
Is there enough space to store nectar? (empty combs/space to build new combs)						
WEATHER						
Temperature/Precipitation						
Has there been a significant change in total population since the last inspection?						

NOTES

INSPECTION CHECKLIST

Date: Time:

	HIVE 1	HIVE 2	HIVE 3	HIVE 4	HIVE 5	HIVE 6
GENERAL HIVE APPEARENCE						
Are the bee actively entering/ exiting the hive?						
Are the bees bringing in pollen?						
Are their signs of robbing?						
Are their signs an animal has been disturbing the hive?						
Are the bees calm when opening the hive? (otherwise it could indicate queenlessness, a poor weather, etc.)						
REPRODUCTION						
Is the brood pattern good? (otherwise it could indicate a disease or an unwell queen)						
Are larvae healthy, shiny and white?						
Is there royal jelly in cells with larva?						
Is there brood in capped or uncapped cells?						
Is there one egg or larva per cell?						
SIGNS OF PEST						
Mites test result (visual inspection only is insufficient)						
Are ants present?						
Are wax moths present?						
Is there an unusual amount of dead bees?						
Is there an odor?						
CAPACITY						
How many frames are covered in bees?						
How many cells are being fully (or almost fully) used for brood?						
Is there enough space to store nectar? (empty combs/space to build new combs)						
WEATHER						
Temperature/Precipitation						
Has there been a significant change in total population since the last inspection?						

NOTES

INSPECTION CHECKLIST

Date: Time:

	HIVE 1	HIVE 2	HIVE 3	HIVE 4	HIVE 5	HIVE 6
GENERAL HIVE APPEARENCE						
Are the bee actively entering/ exiting the hive?						
Are the bees bringing in pollen?						
Are their signs of robbing?						
Are their signs an animal has been disturbing the hive?						
Are the bees calm when opening the hive? (otherwise it could indicate queenlessness, a poor weather, etc.)						
REPRODUCTION						
Is the brood pattern good? (otherwise it could indicate a disease or an unwell queen)						
Are larvae healthy, shiny and white?						
Is there royal jelly in cells with larva?						
Is there brood in capped or uncapped cells?						
Is there one egg or larva per cell?						
SIGNS OF PEST						
Mites test result (visual inspection only is insufficient)						
Are ants present?						
Are wax moths present?						
Is there an unusual amount of dead bees?						
Is there an odor?						
CAPACITY						
How many frames are covered in bees?						
How many cells are being fully (or almost fully) used for brood?						
Is there enough space to store nectar? (empty combs/space to build new combs)						
WEATHER						
Temperature/Precipitation						
Has there been a significant change in total population since the last inspection?						

NOTES

INSPECTION CHECKLIST

Date: Time:

	HIVE 1	HIVE 2	HIVE 3	HIVE 4	HIVE 5	HIVE 6
GENERAL HIVE APPEARENCE						
Are the bee actively entering/ exiting the hive?						
Are the bees bringing in pollen?						
Are their signs of robbing?						
Are their signs an animal has been disturbing the hive?						
Are the bees calm when opening the hive? (otherwise it could indicate queenlessness, a poor weather, etc.)						
REPRODUCTION						
Is the brood pattern good? (otherwise it could indicate a disease or an unwell queen)						
Are larvae healthy, shiny and white?						
Is there royal jelly in cells with larva?						
Is there brood in capped or uncapped cells?						
Is there one egg or larva per cell?						
SIGNS OF PEST						
Mites test result (visual inspection only is insufficient)						
Are ants present?						
Are wax moths present?						
Is there an unusual amount of dead bees?						
Is there an odor?						
CAPACITY						
How many frames are covered in bees?						
How many cells are being fully (or almost fully) used for brood?						
Is there enough space to store nectar? (empty combs/space to build new combs)						
WEATHER						
Temperature/Precipitation						
Has there been a significant change in total population since the last inspection?						

NOTES

INSPECTION CHECKLIST

Date: Time:

	HIVE 1	HIVE 2	HIVE 3	HIVE 4	HIVE 5	HIVE 6
GENERAL HIVE APPEARENCE						
Are the bee actively entering/ exiting the hive?						
Are the bees bringing in pollen?						
Are their signs of robbing?						
Are their signs an animal has been disturbing the hive?						
Are the bees calm when opening the hive? (otherwise it could indicate queenlessness, a poor weather, etc.)						
REPRODUCTION						
Is the brood pattern good? (otherwise it could indicate a disease or an unwell queen)						
Are larvae healthy, shiny and white?						
Is there royal jelly in cells with larva?						
Is there brood in capped or uncapped cells?						
Is there one egg or larva per cell?						
SIGNS OF PEST						
Mites test result (visual inspection only is insufficient)						
Are ants present?						
Are wax moths present?						
Is there an unusual amount of dead bees?						
Is there an odor?						
CAPACITY						
How many frames are covered in bees?						
How many cells are being fully (or almost fully) used for brood?						
Is there enough space to store nectar? (empty combs/space to build new combs)						
WEATHER						
Temperature/Precipitation						
Has there been a significant change in total population since the last inspection?						

NOTES

INSPECTION CHECKLIST

Date: Time:

	HIVE 1	HIVE 2	HIVE 3	HIVE 4	HIVE 5	HIVE 6
GENERAL HIVE APPEARENCE						
Are the bee actively entering/ exiting the hive?						
Are the bees bringing in pollen?						
Are their signs of robbing?						
Are their signs an animal has been disturbing the hive?						
Are the bees calm when opening the hive? (otherwise it could indicate queenlessness, a poor weather, etc.)						
REPRODUCTION						
Is the brood pattern good? (otherwise it could indicate a disease or an unwell queen)						
Are larvae healthy, shiny and white?						
Is there royal jelly in cells with larva?						
Is there brood in capped or uncapped cells?						
Is there one egg or larva per cell?						
SIGNS OF PEST						
Mites test result (visual inspection only is insufficient)						
Are ants present?						
Are wax moths present?						
Is there an unusual amount of dead bees?						
Is there an odor?						
CAPACITY						
How many frames are covered in bees?						
How many cells are being fully (or almost fully) used for brood?						
Is there enough space to store nectar? (empty combs/space to build new combs)						
WEATHER						
Temperature/Precipitation						
Has there been a significant change in total population since the last inspection?						

NOTES

INSPECTION CHECKLIST

Date: Time:

	HIVE 1	HIVE 2	HIVE 3	HIVE 4	HIVE 5	HIVE 6
GENERAL HIVE APPEARENCE						
Are the bee actively entering/ exiting the hive?						
Are the bees bringing in pollen?						
Are their signs of robbing?						
Are their signs an animal has been disturbing the hive?						
Are the bees calm when opening the hive? (otherwise it could indicate queenlessness, a poor weather, etc.)						
REPRODUCTION						
Is the brood pattern good? (otherwise it could indicate a disease or an unwell queen)						
Are larvae healthy, shiny and white?						
Is there royal jelly in cells with larva?						
Is there brood in capped or uncapped cells?						
Is there one egg or larva per cell?						
SIGNS OF PEST						
Mites test result (visual inspection only is insufficient)						
Are ants present?						
Are wax moths present?						
Is there an unusual amount of dead bees?						
Is there an odor?						
CAPACITY						
How many frames are covered in bees?						
How many cells are being fully (or almost fully) used for brood?						
Is there enough space to store nectar? (empty combs/space to build new combs)						
WEATHER						
Temperature/Precipitation						
Has there been a significant change in total population since the last inspection?						

NOTES

INSPECTION CHECKLIST

Date: Time:

	HIVE 1	HIVE 2	HIVE 3	HIVE 4	HIVE 5	HIVE 6
GENERAL HIVE APPEARENCE						
Are the bee actively entering/ exiting the hive?						
Are the bees bringing in pollen?						
Are their signs of robbing?						
Are their signs an animal has been disturbing the hive?						
Are the bees calm when opening the hive? (otherwise it could indicate queenlessness, a poor weather, etc.)						
REPRODUCTION						
Is the brood pattern good? (otherwise it could indicate a disease or an unwell queen)						
Are larvae healthy, shiny and white?						
Is there royal jelly in cells with larva?						
Is there brood in capped or uncapped cells?						
Is there one egg or larva per cell?						
SIGNS OF PEST						
Mites test result (visual inspection only is insufficient)						
Are ants present?						
Are wax moths present?						
Is there an unusual amount of dead bees?						
Is there an odor?						
CAPACITY						
How many frames are covered in bees?						
How many cells are being fully (or almost fully) used for brood?						
Is there enough space to store nectar? (empty combs/space to build new combs)						
WEATHER						
Temperature/Precipitation						
Has there been a significant change in total population since the last inspection?						

NOTES

INSPECTION CHECKLIST

Date: Time:

	HIVE 1	HIVE 2	HIVE 3	HIVE 4	HIVE 5	HIVE 6
GENERAL HIVE APPEARENCE						
Are the bee actively entering/ exiting the hive?						
Are the bees bringing in pollen?						
Are their signs of robbing?						
Are their signs an animal has been disturbing the hive?						
Are the bees calm when opening the hive? (otherwise it could indicate queenlessness, a poor weather, etc.)						
REPRODUCTION						
Is the brood pattern good? (otherwise it could indicate a disease or an unwell queen)						
Are larvae healthy, shiny and white?						
Is there royal jelly in cells with larva?						
Is there brood in capped or uncapped cells?						
Is there one egg or larva per cell?						
SIGNS OF PEST						
Mites test result (visual inspection only is insufficient)						
Are ants present?						
Are wax moths present?						
Is there an unusual amount of dead bees?						
Is there an odor?						
CAPACITY						
How many frames are covered in bees?						
How many cells are being fully (or almost fully) used for brood?						
Is there enough space to store nectar? (empty combs/space to build new combs)						
WEATHER						
Temperature/Precipitation						
Has there been a significant change in total population since the last inspection?						

NOTES

INSPECTION CHECKLIST

Date: Time:

	HIVE 1	HIVE 2	HIVE 3	HIVE 4	HIVE 5	HIVE 6
GENERAL HIVE APPEARENCE						
Are the bee actively entering/ exiting the hive?						
Are the bees bringing in pollen?						
Are their signs of robbing?						
Are their signs an animal has been disturbing the hive?						
Are the bees calm when opening the hive? (otherwise it could indicate queenlessness, a poor weather, etc.)						
REPRODUCTION						
Is the brood pattern good? (otherwise it could indicate a disease or an unwell queen)						
Are larvae healthy, shiny and white?						
Is there royal jelly in cells with larva?						
Is there brood in capped or uncapped cells?						
Is there one egg or larva per cell?						
SIGNS OF PEST						
Mites test result (visual inspection only is insufficient)						
Are ants present?						
Are wax moths present?						
Is there an unusual amount of dead bees?						
Is there an odor?						
CAPACITY						
How many frames are covered in bees?						
How many cells are being fully (or almost fully) used for brood?						
Is there enough space to store nectar? (empty combs/space to build new combs)						
WEATHER						
Temperature/Precipitation						
Has there been a significant change in total population since the last inspection?						

NOTES

INSPECTION CHECKLIST

Date: Time:

	HIVE 1	HIVE 2	HIVE 3	HIVE 4	HIVE 5	HIVE 6
GENERAL HIVE APPEARENCE						
Are the bee actively entering/ exiting the hive?						
Are the bees bringing in pollen?						
Are their signs of robbing?						
Are their signs an animal has been disturbing the hive?						
Are the bees calm when opening the hive? (otherwise it could indicate queenlessness, a poor weather, etc.)						
REPRODUCTION						
Is the brood pattern good? (otherwise it could indicate a disease or an unwell queen)						
Are larvae healthy, shiny and white?						
Is there royal jelly in cells with larva?						
Is there brood in capped or uncapped cells?						
Is there one egg or larva per cell?						
SIGNS OF PEST						
Mites test result (visual inspection only is insufficient)						
Are ants present?						
Are wax moths present?						
Is there an unusual amount of dead bees?						
Is there an odor?						
CAPACITY						
How many frames are covered in bees?						
How many cells are being fully (or almost fully) used for brood?						
Is there enough space to store nectar? (empty combs/space to build new combs)						
WEATHER						
Temperature/Precipitation						
Has there been a significant change in total population since the last inspection?						

NOTES

INSPECTION CHECKLIST

Date: Time:

	HIVE 1	HIVE 2	HIVE 3	HIVE 4	HIVE 5	HIVE 6
GENERAL HIVE APPEARENCE						
Are the bee actively entering/ exiting the hive?						
Are the bees bringing in pollen?						
Are their signs of robbing?						
Are their signs an animal has been disturbing the hive?						
Are the bees calm when opening the hive? (otherwise it could indicate queenlessness, a poor weather, etc.)						
REPRODUCTION						
Is the brood pattern good? (otherwise it could indicate a disease or an unwell queen)						
Are larvae healthy, shiny and white?						
Is there royal jelly in cells with larva?						
Is there brood in capped or uncapped cells?						
Is there one egg or larva per cell?						
SIGNS OF PEST						
Mites test result (visual inspection only is insufficient)						
Are ants present?						
Are wax moths present?						
Is there an unusual amount of dead bees?						
Is there an odor?						
CAPACITY						
How many frames are covered in bees?						
How many cells are being fully (or almost fully) used for brood?						
Is there enough space to store nectar? (empty combs/space to build new combs)						
WEATHER						
Temperature/Precipitation						
Has there been a significant change in total population since the last inspection?						

NOTES

INSPECTION CHECKLIST

Date: Time:

	HIVE 1	HIVE 2	HIVE 3	HIVE 4	HIVE 5	HIVE 6
GENERAL HIVE APPEARENCE						
Are the bee actively entering/ exiting the hive?						
Are the bees bringing in pollen?						
Are their signs of robbing?						
Are their signs an animal has been disturbing the hive?						
Are the bees calm when opening the hive? (otherwise it could indicate queenlessness, a poor weather, etc.)						
REPRODUCTION						
Is the brood pattern good? (otherwise it could indicate a disease or an unwell queen)						
Are larvae healthy, shiny and white?						
Is there royal jelly in cells with larva?						
Is there brood in capped or uncapped cells?						
Is there one egg or larva per cell?						
SIGNS OF PEST						
Mites test result (visual inspection only is insufficient)						
Are ants present?						
Are wax moths present?						
Is there an unusual amount of dead bees?						
Is there an odor?						
CAPACITY						
How many frames are covered in bees?						
How many cells are being fully (or almost fully) used for brood?						
Is there enough space to store nectar? (empty combs/space to build new combs)						
WEATHER						
Temperature/Precipitation						
Has there been a significant change in total population since the last inspection?						

NOTES

INSPECTION CHECKLIST

Date: Time:

	HIVE 1	HIVE 2	HIVE 3	HIVE 4	HIVE 5	HIVE 6
GENERAL HIVE APPEARENCE						
Are the bee actively entering/ exiting the hive?						
Are the bees bringing in pollen?						
Are their signs of robbing?						
Are their signs an animal has been disturbing the hive?						
Are the bees calm when opening the hive? (otherwise it could indicate queenlessness, a poor weather, etc.)						
REPRODUCTION						
Is the brood pattern good? (otherwise it could indicate a disease or an unwell queen)						
Are larvae healthy, shiny and white?						
Is there royal jelly in cells with larva?						
Is there brood in capped or uncapped cells?						
Is there one egg or larva per cell?						
SIGNS OF PEST						
Mites test result (visual inspection only is insufficient)						
Are ants present?						
Are wax moths present?						
Is there an unusual amount of dead bees?						
Is there an odor?						
CAPACITY						
How many frames are covered in bees?						
How many cells are being fully (or almost fully) used for brood?						
Is there enough space to store nectar? (empty combs/space to build new combs)						
WEATHER						
Temperature/Precipitation						
Has there been a significant change in total population since the last inspection?						

NOTES

INSPECTION CHECKLIST

Date: Time:

	HIVE 1	HIVE 2	HIVE 3	HIVE 4	HIVE 5	HIVE 6
GENERAL HIVE APPEARENCE						
Are the bee actively entering/ exiting the hive?						
Are the bees bringing in pollen?						
Are their signs of robbing?						
Are their signs an animal has been disturbing the hive?						
Are the bees calm when opening the hive? (otherwise it could indicate queenlessness, a poor weather, etc.)						
REPRODUCTION						
Is the brood pattern good? (otherwise it could indicate a disease or an unwell queen)						
Are larvae healthy, shiny and white?						
Is there royal jelly in cells with larva?						
Is there brood in capped or uncapped cells?						
Is there one egg or larva per cell?						
SIGNS OF PEST						
Mites test result (visual inspection only is insufficient)						
Are ants present?						
Are wax moths present?						
Is there an unusual amount of dead bees?						
Is there an odor?						
CAPACITY						
How many frames are covered in bees?						
How many cells are being fully (or almost fully) used for brood?						
Is there enough space to store nectar? (empty combs/space to build new combs)						
WEATHER						
Temperature/Precipitation						
Has there been a significant change in total population since the last inspection?						

NOTES

INSPECTION CHECKLIST

Date: Time:

	HIVE 1	HIVE 2	HIVE 3	HIVE 4	HIVE 5	HIVE 6
GENERAL HIVE APPEARENCE						
Are the bee actively entering/ exiting the hive?						
Are the bees bringing in pollen?						
Are their signs of robbing?						
Are their signs an animal has been disturbing the hive?						
Are the bees calm when opening the hive? (otherwise it could indicate queenlessness, a poor weather, etc.)						
REPRODUCTION						
Is the brood pattern good? (otherwise it could indicate a disease or an unwell queen)						
Are larvae healthy, shiny and white?						
Is there royal jelly in cells with larva?						
Is there brood in capped or uncapped cells?						
Is there one egg or larva per cell?						
SIGNS OF PEST						
Mites test result (visual inspection only is insufficient)						
Are ants present?						
Are wax moths present?						
Is there an unusual amount of dead bees?						
Is there an odor?						
CAPACITY						
How many frames are covered in bees?						
How many cells are being fully (or almost fully) used for brood?						
Is there enough space to store nectar? (empty combs/space to build new combs)						
WEATHER						
Temperature/Precipitation						
Has there been a significant change in total population since the last inspection?						

NOTES

INSPECTION CHECKLIST

Date: Time:

	HIVE 1	HIVE 2	HIVE 3	HIVE 4	HIVE 5	HIVE 6
GENERAL HIVE APPEARENCE						
Are the bee actively entering/ exiting the hive?						
Are the bees bringing in pollen?						
Are their signs of robbing?						
Are their signs an animal has been disturbing the hive?						
Are the bees calm when opening the hive? (otherwise it could indicate queenlessness, a poor weather, etc.)						
REPRODUCTION						
Is the brood pattern good? (otherwise it could indicate a disease or an unwell queen)						
Are larvae healthy, shiny and white?						
Is there royal jelly in cells with larva?						
Is there brood in capped or uncapped cells?						
Is there one egg or larva per cell?						
SIGNS OF PEST						
Mites test result (visual inspection only is insufficient)						
Are ants present?						
Are wax moths present?						
Is there an unusual amount of dead bees?						
Is there an odor?						
CAPACITY						
How many frames are covered in bees?						
How many cells are being fully (or almost fully) used for brood?						
Is there enough space to store nectar? (empty combs/space to build new combs)						
WEATHER						
Temperature/Precipitation						
Has there been a significant change in total population since the last inspection?						

NOTES

INSPECTION CHECKLIST

Date: Time:

	HIVE 1	HIVE 2	HIVE 3	HIVE 4	HIVE 5	HIVE 6
GENERAL HIVE APPEARENCE						
Are the bee actively entering/ exiting the hive?						
Are the bees bringing in pollen?						
Are their signs of robbing?						
Are their signs an animal has been disturbing the hive?						
Are the bees calm when opening the hive? (otherwise it could indicate queenlessness, a poor weather, etc.)						
REPRODUCTION						
Is the brood pattern good? (otherwise it could indicate a disease or an unwell queen)						
Are larvae healthy, shiny and white?						
Is there royal jelly in cells with larva?						
Is there brood in capped or uncapped cells?						
Is there one egg or larva per cell?						
SIGNS OF PEST						
Mites test result (visual inspection only is insufficient)						
Are ants present?						
Are wax moths present?						
Is there an unusual amount of dead bees?						
Is there an odor?						
CAPACITY						
How many frames are covered in bees?						
How many cells are being fully (or almost fully) used for brood?						
Is there enough space to store nectar? (empty combs/space to build new combs)						
WEATHER						
Temperature/Precipitation						
Has there been a significant change in total population since the last inspection?						

NOTES

INSPECTION CHECKLIST

Date: Time:

	HIVE 1	HIVE 2	HIVE 3	HIVE 4	HIVE 5	HIVE 6
GENERAL HIVE APPEARENCE						
Are the bee actively entering/ exiting the hive?						
Are the bees bringing in pollen?						
Are their signs of robbing?						
Are their signs an animal has been disturbing the hive?						
Are the bees calm when opening the hive? (otherwise it could indicate queenlessness, a poor weather, etc.)						
REPRODUCTION						
Is the brood pattern good? (otherwise it could indicate a disease or an unwell queen)						
Are larvae healthy, shiny and white?						
Is there royal jelly in cells with larva?						
Is there brood in capped or uncapped cells?						
Is there one egg or larva per cell?						
SIGNS OF PEST						
Mites test result (visual inspection only is insufficient)						
Are ants present?						
Are wax moths present?						
Is there an unusual amount of dead bees?						
Is there an odor?						
CAPACITY						
How many frames are covered in bees?						
How many cells are being fully (or almost fully) used for brood?						
Is there enough space to store nectar? (empty combs/space to build new combs)						
WEATHER						
Temperature/Precipitation						
Has there been a significant change in total population since the last inspection?						

NOTES

INSPECTION CHECKLIST

Date: Time:

	HIVE 1	HIVE 2	HIVE 3	HIVE 4	HIVE 5	HIVE 6
GENERAL HIVE APPEARENCE						
Are the bee actively entering/ exiting the hive?						
Are the bees bringing in pollen?						
Are their signs of robbing?						
Are their signs an animal has been disturbing the hive?						
Are the bees calm when opening the hive? (otherwise it could indicate queenlessness, a poor weather, etc.)						
REPRODUCTION						
Is the brood pattern good? (otherwise it could indicate a disease or an unwell queen)						
Are larvae healthy, shiny and white?						
Is there royal jelly in cells with larva?						
Is there brood in capped or uncapped cells?						
Is there one egg or larva per cell?						
SIGNS OF PEST						
Mites test result (visual inspection only is insufficient)						
Are ants present?						
Are wax moths present?						
Is there an unusual amount of dead bees?						
Is there an odor?						
CAPACITY						
How many frames are covered in bees?						
How many cells are being fully (or almost fully) used for brood?						
Is there enough space to store nectar? (empty combs/space to build new combs)						
WEATHER						
Temperature/Precipitation						
Has there been a significant change in total population since the last inspection?						

NOTES

INSPECTION CHECKLIST

Date: Time:

	HIVE 1	HIVE 2	HIVE 3	HIVE 4	HIVE 5	HIVE 6
GENERAL HIVE APPEARENCE						
Are the bee actively entering/ exiting the hive?						
Are the bees bringing in pollen?						
Are their signs of robbing?						
Are their signs an animal has been disturbing the hive?						
Are the bees calm when opening the hive? (otherwise it could indicate queenlessness, a poor weather, etc.)						
REPRODUCTION						
Is the brood pattern good? (otherwise it could indicate a disease or an unwell queen)						
Are larvae healthy, shiny and white?						
Is there royal jelly in cells with larva?						
Is there brood in capped or uncapped cells?						
Is there one egg or larva per cell?						
SIGNS OF PEST						
Mites test result (visual inspection only is insufficient)						
Are ants present?						
Are wax moths present?						
Is there an unusual amount of dead bees?						
Is there an odor?						
CAPACITY						
How many frames are covered in bees?						
How many cells are being fully (or almost fully) used for brood?						
Is there enough space to store nectar? (empty combs/space to build new combs)						
WEATHER						
Temperature/Precipitation						
Has there been a significant change in total population since the last inspection?						

NOTES

INSPECTION CHECKLIST

Date: Time:

	HIVE 1	HIVE 2	HIVE 3	HIVE 4	HIVE 5	HIVE 6
GENERAL HIVE APPEARENCE						
Are the bee actively entering/ exiting the hive?						
Are the bees bringing in pollen?						
Are their signs of robbing?						
Are their signs an animal has been disturbing the hive?						
Are the bees calm when opening the hive? (otherwise it could indicate queenlessness, a poor weather, etc.)						
REPRODUCTION						
Is the brood pattern good? (otherwise it could indicate a disease or an unwell queen)						
Are larvae healthy, shiny and white?						
Is there royal jelly in cells with larva?						
Is there brood in capped or uncapped cells?						
Is there one egg or larva per cell?						
SIGNS OF PEST						
Mites test result (visual inspection only is insufficient)						
Are ants present?						
Are wax moths present?						
Is there an unusual amount of dead bees?						
Is there an odor?						
CAPACITY						
How many frames are covered in bees?						
How many cells are being fully (or almost fully) used for brood?						
Is there enough space to store nectar? (empty combs/space to build new combs)						
WEATHER						
Temperature/Precipitation						
Has there been a significant change in total population since the last inspection?						

NOTES

INSPECTION CHECKLIST

Date: Time:

	HIVE 1	HIVE 2	HIVE 3	HIVE 4	HIVE 5	HIVE 6
GENERAL HIVE APPEARENCE						
Are the bee actively entering/ exiting the hive?						
Are the bees bringing in pollen?						
Are their signs of robbing?						
Are their signs an animal has been disturbing the hive?						
Are the bees calm when opening the hive? (otherwise it could indicate queenlessness, a poor weather, etc.)						
REPRODUCTION						
Is the brood pattern good? (otherwise it could indicate a disease or an unwell queen)						
Are larvae healthy, shiny and white?						
Is there royal jelly in cells with larva?						
Is there brood in capped or uncapped cells?						
Is there one egg or larva per cell?						
SIGNS OF PEST						
Mites test result (visual inspection only is insufficient)						
Are ants present?						
Are wax moths present?						
Is there an unusual amount of dead bees?						
Is there an odor?						
CAPACITY						
How many frames are covered in bees?						
How many cells are being fully (or almost fully) used for brood?						
Is there enough space to store nectar? (empty combs/space to build new combs)						
WEATHER						
Temperature/Precipitation						
Has there been a significant change in total population since the last inspection?						

NOTES

INSPECTION CHECKLIST

Date: Time:

	HIVE 1	HIVE 2	HIVE 3	HIVE 4	HIVE 5	HIVE 6
GENERAL HIVE APPEARENCE						
Are the bee actively entering/ exiting the hive?						
Are the bees bringing in pollen?						
Are their signs of robbing?						
Are their signs an animal has been disturbing the hive?						
Are the bees calm when opening the hive? (otherwise it could indicate queenlessness, a poor weather, etc.)						
REPRODUCTION						
Is the brood pattern good? (otherwise it could indicate a disease or an unwell queen)						
Are larvae healthy, shiny and white?						
Is there royal jelly in cells with larva?						
Is there brood in capped or uncapped cells?						
Is there one egg or larva per cell?						
SIGNS OF PEST						
Mites test result (visual inspection only is insufficient)						
Are ants present?						
Are wax moths present?						
Is there an unusual amount of dead bees?						
Is there an odor?						
CAPACITY						
How many frames are covered in bees?						
How many cells are being fully (or almost fully) used for brood?						
Is there enough space to store nectar? (empty combs/space to build new combs)						
WEATHER						
Temperature/Precipitation						
Has there been a significant change in total population since the last inspection?						

NOTES

INSPECTION CHECKLIST

Date: Time:

	HIVE 1	HIVE 2	HIVE 3	HIVE 4	HIVE 5	HIVE 6
GENERAL HIVE APPEARENCE						
Are the bee actively entering/ exiting the hive?						
Are the bees bringing in pollen?						
Are their signs of robbing?						
Are their signs an animal has been disturbing the hive?						
Are the bees calm when opening the hive? (otherwise it could indicate queenlessness, a poor weather, etc.)						
REPRODUCTION						
Is the brood pattern good? (otherwise it could indicate a disease or an unwell queen)						
Are larvae healthy, shiny and white?						
Is there royal jelly in cells with larva?						
Is there brood in capped or uncapped cells?						
Is there one egg or larva per cell?						
SIGNS OF PEST						
Mites test result (visual inspection only is insufficient)						
Are ants present?						
Are wax moths present?						
Is there an unusual amount of dead bees?						
Is there an odor?						
CAPACITY						
How many frames are covered in bees?						
How many cells are being fully (or almost fully) used for brood?						
Is there enough space to store nectar? (empty combs/space to build new combs)						
WEATHER						
Temperature/Precipitation						
Has there been a significant change in total population since the last inspection?						

NOTES

INSPECTION CHECKLIST

Date: Time:

	HIVE 1	HIVE 2	HIVE 3	HIVE 4	HIVE 5	HIVE 6
GENERAL HIVE APPEARENCE						
Are the bee actively entering/ exiting the hive?						
Are the bees bringing in pollen?						
Are their signs of robbing?						
Are their signs an animal has been disturbing the hive?						
Are the bees calm when opening the hive? (otherwise it could indicate queenlessness, a poor weather, etc.)						
REPRODUCTION						
Is the brood pattern good? (otherwise it could indicate a disease or an unwell queen)						
Are larvae healthy, shiny and white?						
Is there royal jelly in cells with larva?						
Is there brood in capped or uncapped cells?						
Is there one egg or larva per cell?						
SIGNS OF PEST						
Mites test result (visual inspection only is insufficient)						
Are ants present?						
Are wax moths present?						
Is there an unusual amount of dead bees?						
Is there an odor?						
CAPACITY						
How many frames are covered in bees?						
How many cells are being fully (or almost fully) used for brood?						
Is there enough space to store nectar? (empty combs/space to build new combs)						
WEATHER						
Temperature/Precipitation						
Has there been a significant change in total population since the last inspection?						

NOTES

INSPECTION CHECKLIST

Date: Time:

	HIVE 1	HIVE 2	HIVE 3	HIVE 4	HIVE 5	HIVE 6
GENERAL HIVE APPEARENCE						
Are the bee actively entering/ exiting the hive?						
Are the bees bringing in pollen?						
Are their signs of robbing?						
Are their signs an animal has been disturbing the hive?						
Are the bees calm when opening the hive? (otherwise it could indicate queenlessness, a poor weather, etc.)						
REPRODUCTION						
Is the brood pattern good? (otherwise it could indicate a disease or an unwell queen)						
Are larvae healthy, shiny and white?						
Is there royal jelly in cells with larva?						
Is there brood in capped or uncapped cells?						
Is there one egg or larva per cell?						
SIGNS OF PEST						
Mites test result (visual inspection only is insufficient)						
Are ants present?						
Are wax moths present?						
Is there an unusual amount of dead bees?						
Is there an odor?						
CAPACITY						
How many frames are covered in bees?						
How many cells are being fully (or almost fully) used for brood?						
Is there enough space to store nectar? (empty combs/space to build new combs)						
WEATHER						
Temperature/Precipitation						
Has there been a significant change in total population since the last inspection?						

NOTES

INSPECTION CHECKLIST

Date: Time:

	HIVE 1	HIVE 2	HIVE 3	HIVE 4	HIVE 5	HIVE 6
GENERAL HIVE APPEARENCE						
Are the bee actively entering/ exiting the hive?						
Are the bees bringing in pollen?						
Are their signs of robbing?						
Are their signs an animal has been disturbing the hive?						
Are the bees calm when opening the hive? (otherwise it could indicate queenlessness, a poor weather, etc.)						
REPRODUCTION						
Is the brood pattern good? (otherwise it could indicate a disease or an unwell queen)						
Are larvae healthy, shiny and white?						
Is there royal jelly in cells with larva?						
Is there brood in capped or uncapped cells?						
Is there one egg or larva per cell?						
SIGNS OF PEST						
Mites test result (visual inspection only is insufficient)						
Are ants present?						
Are wax moths present?						
Is there an unusual amount of dead bees?						
Is there an odor?						
CAPACITY						
How many frames are covered in bees?						
How many cells are being fully (or almost fully) used for brood?						
Is there enough space to store nectar? (empty combs/space to build new combs)						
WEATHER						
Temperature/Precipitation						
Has there been a significant change in total population since the last inspection?						

NOTES

INSPECTION CHECKLIST

Date: Time:

	HIVE 1	HIVE 2	HIVE 3	HIVE 4	HIVE 5	HIVE 6
GENERAL HIVE APPEARENCE						
Are the bee actively entering/ exiting the hive?						
Are the bees bringing in pollen?						
Are their signs of robbing?						
Are their signs an animal has been disturbing the hive?						
Are the bees calm when opening the hive? (otherwise it could indicate queenlessness, a poor weather, etc.)						
REPRODUCTION						
Is the brood pattern good? (otherwise it could indicate a disease or an unwell queen)						
Are larvae healthy, shiny and white?						
Is there royal jelly in cells with larva?						
Is there brood in capped or uncapped cells?						
Is there one egg or larva per cell?						
SIGNS OF PEST						
Mites test result (visual inspection only is insufficient)						
Are ants present?						
Are wax moths present?						
Is there an unusual amount of dead bees?						
Is there an odor?						
CAPACITY						
How many frames are covered in bees?						
How many cells are being fully (or almost fully) used for brood?						
Is there enough space to store nectar? (empty combs/space to build new combs)						
WEATHER						
Temperature/Precipitation						
Has there been a significant change in total population since the last inspection?						

NOTES

INSPECTION CHECKLIST

Date: Time:

	HIVE 1	HIVE 2	HIVE 3	HIVE 4	HIVE 5	HIVE 6
GENERAL HIVE APPEARENCE						
Are the bee actively entering/ exiting the hive?						
Are the bees bringing in pollen?						
Are their signs of robbing?						
Are their signs an animal has been disturbing the hive?						
Are the bees calm when opening the hive? (otherwise it could indicate queenlessness, a poor weather, etc.)						
REPRODUCTION						
Is the brood pattern good? (otherwise it could indicate a disease or an unwell queen)						
Are larvae healthy, shiny and white?						
Is there royal jelly in cells with larva?						
Is there brood in capped or uncapped cells?						
Is there one egg or larva per cell?						
SIGNS OF PEST						
Mites test result (visual inspection only is insufficient)						
Are ants present?						
Are wax moths present?						
Is there an unusual amount of dead bees?						
Is there an odor?						
CAPACITY						
How many frames are covered in bees?						
How many cells are being fully (or almost fully) used for brood?						
Is there enough space to store nectar? (empty combs/space to build new combs)						
WEATHER						
Temperature/Precipitation						
Has there been a significant change in total population since the last inspection?						

NOTES

INSPECTION CHECKLIST

Date: Time:

	HIVE 1	HIVE 2	HIVE 3	HIVE 4	HIVE 5	HIVE 6
GENERAL HIVE APPEARENCE						
Are the bee actively entering/ exiting the hive?						
Are the bees bringing in pollen?						
Are their signs of robbing?						
Are their signs an animal has been disturbing the hive?						
Are the bees calm when opening the hive? (otherwise it could indicate queenlessness, a poor weather, etc.)						
REPRODUCTION						
Is the brood pattern good? (otherwise it could indicate a disease or an unwell queen)						
Are larvae healthy, shiny and white?						
Is there royal jelly in cells with larva?						
Is there brood in capped or uncapped cells?						
Is there one egg or larva per cell?						
SIGNS OF PEST						
Mites test result (visual inspection only is insufficient)						
Are ants present?						
Are wax moths present?						
Is there an unusual amount of dead bees?						
Is there an odor?						
CAPACITY						
How many frames are covered in bees?						
How many cells are being fully (or almost fully) used for brood?						
Is there enough space to store nectar? (empty combs/space to build new combs)						
WEATHER						
Temperature/Precipitation						
Has there been a significant change in total population since the last inspection?						

NOTES

INSPECTION CHECKLIST

Date: Time:

	HIVE 1	HIVE 2	HIVE 3	HIVE 4	HIVE 5	HIVE 6
GENERAL HIVE APPEARENCE						
Are the bee actively entering/ exiting the hive?						
Are the bees bringing in pollen?						
Are their signs of robbing?						
Are their signs an animal has been disturbing the hive?						
Are the bees calm when opening the hive? (otherwise it could indicate queenlessness, a poor weather, etc.)						
REPRODUCTION						
Is the brood pattern good? (otherwise it could indicate a disease or an unwell queen)						
Are larvae healthy, shiny and white?						
Is there royal jelly in cells with larva?						
Is there brood in capped or uncapped cells?						
Is there one egg or larva per cell?						
SIGNS OF PEST						
Mites test result (visual inspection only is insufficient)						
Are ants present?						
Are wax moths present?						
Is there an unusual amount of dead bees?						
Is there an odor?						
CAPACITY						
How many frames are covered in bees?						
How many cells are being fully (or almost fully) used for brood?						
Is there enough space to store nectar? (empty combs/space to build new combs)						
WEATHER						
Temperature/Precipitation						
Has there been a significant change in total population since the last inspection?						

NOTES

INSPECTION CHECKLIST

Date: Time:

	HIVE 1	HIVE 2	HIVE 3	HIVE 4	HIVE 5	HIVE 6
GENERAL HIVE APPEARENCE						
Are the bee actively entering/ exiting the hive?						
Are the bees bringing in pollen?						
Are their signs of robbing?						
Are their signs an animal has been disturbing the hive?						
Are the bees calm when opening the hive? (otherwise it could indicate queenlessness, a poor weather, etc.)						
REPRODUCTION						
Is the brood pattern good? (otherwise it could indicate a disease or an unwell queen)						
Are larvae healthy, shiny and white?						
Is there royal jelly in cells with larva?						
Is there brood in capped or uncapped cells?						
Is there one egg or larva per cell?						
SIGNS OF PEST						
Mites test result (visual inspection only is insufficient)						
Are ants present?						
Are wax moths present?						
Is there an unusual amount of dead bees?						
Is there an odor?						
CAPACITY						
How many frames are covered in bees?						
How many cells are being fully (or almost fully) used for brood?						
Is there enough space to store nectar? (empty combs/space to build new combs)						
WEATHER						
Temperature/Precipitation						
Has there been a significant change in total population since the last inspection?						

NOTES

INSPECTION CHECKLIST

Date: Time:

	HIVE 1	HIVE 2	HIVE 3	HIVE 4	HIVE 5	HIVE 6
GENERAL HIVE APPEARENCE						
Are the bee actively entering/ exiting the hive?						
Are the bees bringing in pollen?						
Are their signs of robbing?						
Are their signs an animal has been disturbing the hive?						
Are the bees calm when opening the hive? (otherwise it could indicate queenlessness, a poor weather, etc.)						
REPRODUCTION						
Is the brood pattern good? (otherwise it could indicate a disease or an unwell queen)						
Are larvae healthy, shiny and white?						
Is there royal jelly in cells with larva?						
Is there brood in capped or uncapped cells?						
Is there one egg or larva per cell?						
SIGNS OF PEST						
Mites test result (visual inspection only is insufficient)						
Are ants present?						
Are wax moths present?						
Is there an unusual amount of dead bees?						
Is there an odor?						
CAPACITY						
How many frames are covered in bees?						
How many cells are being fully (or almost fully) used for brood?						
Is there enough space to store nectar? (empty combs/space to build new combs)						
WEATHER						
Temperature/Precipitation						
Has there been a significant change in total population since the last inspection?						

NOTES

INSPECTION CHECKLIST

Date: Time:

	HIVE 1	HIVE 2	HIVE 3	HIVE 4	HIVE 5	HIVE 6
GENERAL HIVE APPEARENCE						
Are the bee actively entering/ exiting the hive?						
Are the bees bringing in pollen?						
Are their signs of robbing?						
Are their signs an animal has been disturbing the hive?						
Are the bees calm when opening the hive? (otherwise it could indicate queenlessness, a poor weather, etc.)						
REPRODUCTION						
Is the brood pattern good? (otherwise it could indicate a disease or an unwell queen)						
Are larvae healthy, shiny and white?						
Is there royal jelly in cells with larva?						
Is there brood in capped or uncapped cells?						
Is there one egg or larva per cell?						
SIGNS OF PEST						
Mites test result (visual inspection only is insufficient)						
Are ants present?						
Are wax moths present?						
Is there an unusual amount of dead bees?						
Is there an odor?						
CAPACITY						
How many frames are covered in bees?						
How many cells are being fully (or almost fully) used for brood?						
Is there enough space to store nectar? (empty combs/space to build new combs)						
WEATHER						
Temperature/Precipitation						
Has there been a significant change in total population since the last inspection?						

NOTES

INSPECTION CHECKLIST

Date: Time:

	HIVE 1	HIVE 2	HIVE 3	HIVE 4	HIVE 5	HIVE 6
GENERAL HIVE APPEARENCE						
Are the bee actively entering/ exiting the hive?						
Are the bees bringing in pollen?						
Are their signs of robbing?						
Are their signs an animal has been disturbing the hive?						
Are the bees calm when opening the hive? (otherwise it could indicate queenlessness, a poor weather, etc.)						
REPRODUCTION						
Is the brood pattern good? (otherwise it could indicate a disease or an unwell queen)						
Are larvae healthy, shiny and white?						
Is there royal jelly in cells with larva?						
Is there brood in capped or uncapped cells?						
Is there one egg or larva per cell?						
SIGNS OF PEST						
Mites test result (visual inspection only is insufficient)						
Are ants present?						
Are wax moths present?						
Is there an unusual amount of dead bees?						
Is there an odor?						
CAPACITY						
How many frames are covered in bees?						
How many cells are being fully (or almost fully) used for brood?						
Is there enough space to store nectar? (empty combs/space to build new combs)						
WEATHER						
Temperature/Precipitation						
Has there been a significant change in total population since the last inspection?						

NOTES

INSPECTION CHECKLIST

Date: Time:

	HIVE 1	HIVE 2	HIVE 3	HIVE 4	HIVE 5	HIVE 6
GENERAL HIVE APPEARENCE						
Are the bee actively entering/ exiting the hive?						
Are the bees bringing in pollen?						
Are their signs of robbing?						
Are their signs an animal has been disturbing the hive?						
Are the bees calm when opening the hive? (otherwise it could indicate queenlessness, a poor weather, etc.)						
REPRODUCTION						
Is the brood pattern good? (otherwise it could indicate a disease or an unwell queen)						
Are larvae healthy, shiny and white?						
Is there royal jelly in cells with larva?						
Is there brood in capped or uncapped cells?						
Is there one egg or larva per cell?						
SIGNS OF PEST						
Mites test result (visual inspection only is insufficient)						
Are ants present?						
Are wax moths present?						
Is there an unusual amount of dead bees?						
Is there an odor?						
CAPACITY						
How many frames are covered in bees?						
How many cells are being fully (or almost fully) used for brood?						
Is there enough space to store nectar? (empty combs/space to build new combs)						
WEATHER						
Temperature/Precipitation						
Has there been a significant change in total population since the last inspection?						

NOTES

INSPECTION CHECKLIST

Date: Time:

	HIVE 1	HIVE 2	HIVE 3	HIVE 4	HIVE 5	HIVE 6
GENERAL HIVE APPEARENCE						
Are the bee actively entering/ exiting the hive?						
Are the bees bringing in pollen?						
Are their signs of robbing?						
Are their signs an animal has been disturbing the hive?						
Are the bees calm when opening the hive? (otherwise it could indicate queenlessness, a poor weather, etc.)						
REPRODUCTION						
Is the brood pattern good? (otherwise it could indicate a disease or an unwell queen)						
Are larvae healthy, shiny and white?						
Is there royal jelly in cells with larva?						
Is there brood in capped or uncapped cells?						
Is there one egg or larva per cell?						
SIGNS OF PEST						
Mites test result (visual inspection only is insufficient)						
Are ants present?						
Are wax moths present?						
Is there an unusual amount of dead bees?						
Is there an odor?						
CAPACITY						
How many frames are covered in bees?						
How many cells are being fully (or almost fully) used for brood?						
Is there enough space to store nectar? (empty combs/space to build new combs)						
WEATHER						
Temperature/Precipitation						
Has there been a significant change in total population since the last inspection?						

NOTES

INSPECTION CHECKLIST

Date: Time:

	HIVE 1	HIVE 2	HIVE 3	HIVE 4	HIVE 5	HIVE 6
GENERAL HIVE APPEARENCE						
Are the bee actively entering/ exiting the hive?						
Are the bees bringing in pollen?						
Are their signs of robbing?						
Are their signs an animal has been disturbing the hive?						
Are the bees calm when opening the hive? (otherwise it could indicate queenlessness, a poor weather, etc.)						
REPRODUCTION						
Is the brood pattern good? (otherwise it could indicate a disease or an unwell queen)						
Are larvae healthy, shiny and white?						
Is there royal jelly in cells with larva?						
Is there brood in capped or uncapped cells?						
Is there one egg or larva per cell?						
SIGNS OF PEST						
Mites test result (visual inspection only is insufficient)						
Are ants present?						
Are wax moths present?						
Is there an unusual amount of dead bees?						
Is there an odor?						
CAPACITY						
How many frames are covered in bees?						
How many cells are being fully (or almost fully) used for brood?						
Is there enough space to store nectar? (empty combs/space to build new combs)						
WEATHER						
Temperature/Precipitation						
Has there been a significant change in total population since the last inspection?						

NOTES

INSPECTION CHECKLIST

Date: Time:

	HIVE 1	HIVE 2	HIVE 3	HIVE 4	HIVE 5	HIVE 6
GENERAL HIVE APPEARENCE						
Are the bee actively entering/ exiting the hive?						
Are the bees bringing in pollen?						
Are their signs of robbing?						
Are their signs an animal has been disturbing the hive?						
Are the bees calm when opening the hive? (otherwise it could indicate queenlessness, a poor weather, etc.)						
REPRODUCTION						
Is the brood pattern good? (otherwise it could indicate a disease or an unwell queen)						
Are larvae healthy, shiny and white?						
Is there royal jelly in cells with larva?						
Is there brood in capped or uncapped cells?						
Is there one egg or larva per cell?						
SIGNS OF PEST						
Mites test result (visual inspection only is insufficient)						
Are ants present?						
Are wax moths present?						
Is there an unusual amount of dead bees?						
Is there an odor?						
CAPACITY						
How many frames are covered in bees?						
How many cells are being fully (or almost fully) used for brood?						
Is there enough space to store nectar? (empty combs/space to build new combs)						
WEATHER						
Temperature/Precipitation						
Has there been a significant change in total population since the last inspection?						

NOTES

INSPECTION CHECKLIST

Date: Time:

	HIVE 1	HIVE 2	HIVE 3	HIVE 4	HIVE 5	HIVE 6
GENERAL HIVE APPEARENCE						
Are the bee actively entering/ exiting the hive?						
Are the bees bringing in pollen?						
Are their signs of robbing?						
Are their signs an animal has been disturbing the hive?						
Are the bees calm when opening the hive? (otherwise it could indicate queenlessness, a poor weather, etc.)						
REPRODUCTION						
Is the brood pattern good? (otherwise it could indicate a disease or an unwell queen)						
Are larvae healthy, shiny and white?						
Is there royal jelly in cells with larva?						
Is there brood in capped or uncapped cells?						
Is there one egg or larva per cell?						
SIGNS OF PEST						
Mites test result (visual inspection only is insufficient)						
Are ants present?						
Are wax moths present?						
Is there an unusual amount of dead bees?						
Is there an odor?						
CAPACITY						
How many frames are covered in bees?						
How many cells are being fully (or almost fully) used for brood?						
Is there enough space to store nectar? (empty combs/space to build new combs)						
WEATHER						
Temperature/Precipitation						
Has there been a significant change in total population since the last inspection?						

NOTES

INSPECTION CHECKLIST

Date: Time:

	HIVE 1	HIVE 2	HIVE 3	HIVE 4	HIVE 5	HIVE 6
GENERAL HIVE APPEARENCE						
Are the bee actively entering/ exiting the hive?						
Are the bees bringing in pollen?						
Are their signs of robbing?						
Are their signs an animal has been disturbing the hive?						
Are the bees calm when opening the hive? (otherwise it could indicate queenlessness, a poor weather, etc.)						
REPRODUCTION						
Is the brood pattern good? (otherwise it could indicate a disease or an unwell queen)						
Are larvae healthy, shiny and white?						
Is there royal jelly in cells with larva?						
Is there brood in capped or uncapped cells?						
Is there one egg or larva per cell?						
SIGNS OF PEST						
Mites test result (visual inspection only is insufficient)						
Are ants present?						
Are wax moths present?						
Is there an unusual amount of dead bees?						
Is there an odor?						
CAPACITY						
How many frames are covered in bees?						
How many cells are being fully (or almost fully) used for brood?						
Is there enough space to store nectar? (empty combs/space to build new combs)						
WEATHER						
Temperature/Precipitation						
Has there been a significant change in total population since the last inspection?						

NOTES

INSPECTION CHECKLIST

Date: Time:

	HIVE 1	HIVE 2	HIVE 3	HIVE 4	HIVE 5	HIVE 6
GENERAL HIVE APPEARENCE						
Are the bee actively entering/ exiting the hive?						
Are the bees bringing in pollen?						
Are their signs of robbing?						
Are their signs an animal has been disturbing the hive?						
Are the bees calm when opening the hive? (otherwise it could indicate queenlessness, a poor weather, etc.)						
REPRODUCTION						
Is the brood pattern good? (otherwise it could indicate a disease or an unwell queen)						
Are larvae healthy, shiny and white?						
Is there royal jelly in cells with larva?						
Is there brood in capped or uncapped cells?						
Is there one egg or larva per cell?						
SIGNS OF PEST						
Mites test result (visual inspection only is insufficient)						
Are ants present?						
Are wax moths present?						
Is there an unusual amount of dead bees?						
Is there an odor?						
CAPACITY						
How many frames are covered in bees?						
How many cells are being fully (or almost fully) used for brood?						
Is there enough space to store nectar? (empty combs/space to build new combs)						
WEATHER						
Temperature/Precipitation						
Has there been a significant change in total population since the last inspection?						

NOTES

INSPECTION CHECKLIST

Date: Time:

	HIVE 1	HIVE 2	HIVE 3	HIVE 4	HIVE 5	HIVE 6
GENERAL HIVE APPEARENCE						
Are the bee actively entering/ exiting the hive?						
Are the bees bringing in pollen?						
Are their signs of robbing?						
Are their signs an animal has been disturbing the hive?						
Are the bees calm when opening the hive? (otherwise it could indicate queenlessness, a poor weather, etc.)						
REPRODUCTION						
Is the brood pattern good? (otherwise it could indicate a disease or an unwell queen)						
Are larvae healthy, shiny and white?						
Is there royal jelly in cells with larva?						
Is there brood in capped or uncapped cells?						
Is there one egg or larva per cell?						
SIGNS OF PEST						
Mites test result (visual inspection only is insufficient)						
Are ants present?						
Are wax moths present?						
Is there an unusual amount of dead bees?						
Is there an odor?						
CAPACITY						
How many frames are covered in bees?						
How many cells are being fully (or almost fully) used for brood?						
Is there enough space to store nectar? (empty combs/space to build new combs)						
WEATHER						
Temperature/Precipitation						
Has there been a significant change in total population since the last inspection?						

NOTES

INSPECTION CHECKLIST

Date: Time:

	HIVE 1	HIVE 2	HIVE 3	HIVE 4	HIVE 5	HIVE 6
GENERAL HIVE APPEARENCE						
Are the bee actively entering/ exiting the hive?						
Are the bees bringing in pollen?						
Are their signs of robbing?						
Are their signs an animal has been disturbing the hive?						
Are the bees calm when opening the hive? (otherwise it could indicate queenlessness, a poor weather, etc.)						
REPRODUCTION						
Is the brood pattern good? (otherwise it could indicate a disease or an unwell queen)						
Are larvae healthy, shiny and white?						
Is there royal jelly in cells with larva?						
Is there brood in capped or uncapped cells?						
Is there one egg or larva per cell?						
SIGNS OF PEST						
Mites test result (visual inspection only is insufficient)						
Are ants present?						
Are wax moths present?						
Is there an unusual amount of dead bees?						
Is there an odor?						
CAPACITY						
How many frames are covered in bees?						
How many cells are being fully (or almost fully) used for brood?						
Is there enough space to store nectar? (empty combs/space to build new combs)						
WEATHER						
Temperature/Precipitation						
Has there been a significant change in total population since the last inspection?						

NOTES

INSPECTION CHECKLIST

Date: Time:

	HIVE 1	HIVE 2	HIVE 3	HIVE 4	HIVE 5	HIVE 6
GENERAL HIVE APPEARENCE						
Are the bee actively entering/ exiting the hive?						
Are the bees bringing in pollen?						
Are their signs of robbing?						
Are their signs an animal has been disturbing the hive?						
Are the bees calm when opening the hive? (otherwise it could indicate queenlessness, a poor weather, etc.)						
REPRODUCTION						
Is the brood pattern good? (otherwise it could indicate a disease or an unwell queen)						
Are larvae healthy, shiny and white?						
Is there royal jelly in cells with larva?						
Is there brood in capped or uncapped cells?						
Is there one egg or larva per cell?						
SIGNS OF PEST						
Mites test result (visual inspection only is insufficient)						
Are ants present?						
Are wax moths present?						
Is there an unusual amount of dead bees?						
Is there an odor?						
CAPACITY						
How many frames are covered in bees?						
How many cells are being fully (or almost fully) used for brood?						
Is there enough space to store nectar? (empty combs/space to build new combs)						
WEATHER						
Temperature/Precipitation						
Has there been a significant change in total population since the last inspection?						

NOTES

INSPECTION CHECKLIST

Date: Time:

	HIVE 1	HIVE 2	HIVE 3	HIVE 4	HIVE 5	HIVE 6
GENERAL HIVE APPEARENCE						
Are the bee actively entering/ exiting the hive?						
Are the bees bringing in pollen?						
Are their signs of robbing?						
Are their signs an animal has been disturbing the hive?						
Are the bees calm when opening the hive? (otherwise it could indicate queenlessness, a poor weather, etc.)						
REPRODUCTION						
Is the brood pattern good? (otherwise it could indicate a disease or an unwell queen)						
Are larvae healthy, shiny and white?						
Is there royal jelly in cells with larva?						
Is there brood in capped or uncapped cells?						
Is there one egg or larva per cell?						
SIGNS OF PEST						
Mites test result (visual inspection only is insufficient)						
Are ants present?						
Are wax moths present?						
Is there an unusual amount of dead bees?						
Is there an odor?						
CAPACITY						
How many frames are covered in bees?						
How many cells are being fully (or almost fully) used for brood?						
Is there enough space to store nectar? (empty combs/space to build new combs)						
WEATHER						
Temperature/Precipitation						
Has there been a significant change in total population since the last inspection?						

NOTES

INSPECTION CHECKLIST

Date: Time:

	HIVE 1	HIVE 2	HIVE 3	HIVE 4	HIVE 5	HIVE 6
GENERAL HIVE APPEARENCE						
Are the bee actively entering/ exiting the hive?						
Are the bees bringing in pollen?						
Are their signs of robbing?						
Are their signs an animal has been disturbing the hive?						
Are the bees calm when opening the hive? (otherwise it could indicate queenlessness, a poor weather, etc.)						
REPRODUCTION						
Is the brood pattern good? (otherwise it could indicate a disease or an unwell queen)						
Are larvae healthy, shiny and white?						
Is there royal jelly in cells with larva?						
Is there brood in capped or uncapped cells?						
Is there one egg or larva per cell?						
SIGNS OF PEST						
Mites test result (visual inspection only is insufficient)						
Are ants present?						
Are wax moths present?						
Is there an unusual amount of dead bees?						
Is there an odor?						
CAPACITY						
How many frames are covered in bees?						
How many cells are being fully (or almost fully) used for brood?						
Is there enough space to store nectar? (empty combs/space to build new combs)						
WEATHER						
Temperature/Precipitation						
Has there been a significant change in total population since the last inspection?						

NOTES

INSPECTION CHECKLIST

Date: Time:

	HIVE 1	HIVE 2	HIVE 3	HIVE 4	HIVE 5	HIVE 6
GENERAL HIVE APPEARENCE						
Are the bee actively entering/ exiting the hive?						
Are the bees bringing in pollen?						
Are their signs of robbing?						
Are their signs an animal has been disturbing the hive?						
Are the bees calm when opening the hive? (otherwise it could indicate queenlessness, a poor weather, etc.)						
REPRODUCTION						
Is the brood pattern good? (otherwise it could indicate a disease or an unwell queen)						
Are larvae healthy, shiny and white?						
Is there royal jelly in cells with larva?						
Is there brood in capped or uncapped cells?						
Is there one egg or larva per cell?						
SIGNS OF PEST						
Mites test result (visual inspection only is insufficient)						
Are ants present?						
Are wax moths present?						
Is there an unusual amount of dead bees?						
Is there an odor?						
CAPACITY						
How many frames are covered in bees?						
How many cells are being fully (or almost fully) used for brood?						
Is there enough space to store nectar? (empty combs/space to build new combs)						
WEATHER						
Temperature/Precipitation						
Has there been a significant change in total population since the last inspection?						

NOTES

INSPECTION CHECKLIST

Date: Time:

	HIVE 1	HIVE 2	HIVE 3	HIVE 4	HIVE 5	HIVE 6
GENERAL HIVE APPEARENCE						
Are the bee actively entering/ exiting the hive?						
Are the bees bringing in pollen?						
Are their signs of robbing?						
Are their signs an animal has been disturbing the hive?						
Are the bees calm when opening the hive? (otherwise it could indicate queenlessness, a poor weather, etc.)						
REPRODUCTION						
Is the brood pattern good? (otherwise it could indicate a disease or an unwell queen)						
Are larvae healthy, shiny and white?						
Is there royal jelly in cells with larva?						
Is there brood in capped or uncapped cells?						
Is there one egg or larva per cell?						
SIGNS OF PEST						
Mites test result (visual inspection only is insufficient)						
Are ants present?						
Are wax moths present?						
Is there an unusual amount of dead bees?						
Is there an odor?						
CAPACITY						
How many frames are covered in bees?						
How many cells are being fully (or almost fully) used for brood?						
Is there enough space to store nectar? (empty combs/space to build new combs)						
WEATHER						
Temperature/Precipitation						
Has there been a significant change in total population since the last inspection?						

NOTES

INSPECTION CHECKLIST

Date: Time:

	HIVE 1	HIVE 2	HIVE 3	HIVE 4	HIVE 5	HIVE 6
GENERAL HIVE APPEARENCE						
Are the bee actively entering/ exiting the hive?						
Are the bees bringing in pollen?						
Are their signs of robbing?						
Are their signs an animal has been disturbing the hive?						
Are the bees calm when opening the hive? (otherwise it could indicate queenlessness, a poor weather, etc.)						
REPRODUCTION						
Is the brood pattern good? (otherwise it could indicate a disease or an unwell queen)						
Are larvae healthy, shiny and white?						
Is there royal jelly in cells with larva?						
Is there brood in capped or uncapped cells?						
Is there one egg or larva per cell?						
SIGNS OF PEST						
Mites test result (visual inspection only is insufficient)						
Are ants present?						
Are wax moths present?						
Is there an unusual amount of dead bees?						
Is there an odor?						
CAPACITY						
How many frames are covered in bees?						
How many cells are being fully (or almost fully) used for brood?						
Is there enough space to store nectar? (empty combs/space to build new combs)						
WEATHER						
Temperature/Precipitation						
Has there been a significant change in total population since the last inspection?						

NOTES

INSPECTION CHECKLIST

Date: Time:

	HIVE 1	HIVE 2	HIVE 3	HIVE 4	HIVE 5	HIVE 6
GENERAL HIVE APPEARENCE						
Are the bee actively entering/ exiting the hive?						
Are the bees bringing in pollen?						
Are their signs of robbing?						
Are their signs an animal has been disturbing the hive?						
Are the bees calm when opening the hive? (otherwise it could indicate queenlessness, a poor weather, etc.)						
REPRODUCTION						
Is the brood pattern good? (otherwise it could indicate a disease or an unwell queen)						
Are larvae healthy, shiny and white?						
Is there royal jelly in cells with larva?						
Is there brood in capped or uncapped cells?						
Is there one egg or larva per cell?						
SIGNS OF PEST						
Mites test result (visual inspection only is insufficient)						
Are ants present?						
Are wax moths present?						
Is there an unusual amount of dead bees?						
Is there an odor?						
CAPACITY						
How many frames are covered in bees?						
How many cells are being fully (or almost fully) used for brood?						
Is there enough space to store nectar? (empty combs/space to build new combs)						
WEATHER						
Temperature/Precipitation						
Has there been a significant change in total population since the last inspection?						

NOTES

INSPECTION CHECKLIST

Date: Time:

	HIVE 1	HIVE 2	HIVE 3	HIVE 4	HIVE 5	HIVE 6
GENERAL HIVE APPEARENCE						
Are the bee actively entering/ exiting the hive?						
Are the bees bringing in pollen?						
Are their signs of robbing?						
Are their signs an animal has been disturbing the hive?						
Are the bees calm when opening the hive? (otherwise it could indicate queenlessness, a poor weather, etc.)						
REPRODUCTION						
Is the brood pattern good? (otherwise it could indicate a disease or an unwell queen)						
Are larvae healthy, shiny and white?						
Is there royal jelly in cells with larva?						
Is there brood in capped or uncapped cells?						
Is there one egg or larva per cell?						
SIGNS OF PEST						
Mites test result (visual inspection only is insufficient)						
Are ants present?						
Are wax moths present?						
Is there an unusual amount of dead bees?						
Is there an odor?						
CAPACITY						
How many frames are covered in bees?						
How many cells are being fully (or almost fully) used for brood?						
Is there enough space to store nectar? (empty combs/space to build new combs)						
WEATHER						
Temperature/Precipitation						
Has there been a significant change in total population since the last inspection?						

NOTES

INSPECTION CHECKLIST

Date: Time:

	HIVE 1	HIVE 2	HIVE 3	HIVE 4	HIVE 5	HIVE 6
GENERAL HIVE APPEARENCE						
Are the bee actively entering/ exiting the hive?						
Are the bees bringing in pollen?						
Are their signs of robbing?						
Are their signs an animal has been disturbing the hive?						
Are the bees calm when opening the hive? (otherwise it could indicate queenlessness, a poor weather, etc.)						
REPRODUCTION						
Is the brood pattern good? (otherwise it could indicate a disease or an unwell queen)						
Are larvae healthy, shiny and white?						
Is there royal jelly in cells with larva?						
Is there brood in capped or uncapped cells?						
Is there one egg or larva per cell?						
SIGNS OF PEST						
Mites test result (visual inspection only is insufficient)						
Are ants present?						
Are wax moths present?						
Is there an unusual amount of dead bees?						
Is there an odor?						
CAPACITY						
How many frames are covered in bees?						
How many cells are being fully (or almost fully) used for brood?						
Is there enough space to store nectar? (empty combs/space to build new combs)						
WEATHER						
Temperature/Precipitation						
Has there been a significant change in total population since the last inspection?						

NOTES

INSPECTION CHECKLIST

Date: Time:

	HIVE 1	HIVE 2	HIVE 3	HIVE 4	HIVE 5	HIVE 6
GENERAL HIVE APPEARENCE						
Are the bee actively entering/ exiting the hive?						
Are the bees bringing in pollen?						
Are their signs of robbing?						
Are their signs an animal has been disturbing the hive?						
Are the bees calm when opening the hive? (otherwise it could indicate queenlessness, a poor weather, etc.)						
REPRODUCTION						
Is the brood pattern good? (otherwise it could indicate a disease or an unwell queen)						
Are larvae healthy, shiny and white?						
Is there royal jelly in cells with larva?						
Is there brood in capped or uncapped cells?						
Is there one egg or larva per cell?						
SIGNS OF PEST						
Mites test result (visual inspection only is insufficient)						
Are ants present?						
Are wax moths present?						
Is there an unusual amount of dead bees?						
Is there an odor?						
CAPACITY						
How many frames are covered in bees?						
How many cells are being fully (or almost fully) used for brood?						
Is there enough space to store nectar? (empty combs/space to build new combs)						
WEATHER						
Temperature/Precipitation						
Has there been a significant change in total population since the last inspection?						

NOTES

Made in the USA
Monee, IL
26 March 2021

63928236R00072